ASTERISM

The Dorset Prize for Poetry

Ae Hee Lee, *Asterism*
  Selected by John Murillo

Teresa Dzieglewicz, *Something Small of
  How to See a River* Selected by Tyehimba Jess

Meredith Stricker, *Rewild*
  Selected by Maggie Smith

Lisa Hiton, *Afterfeast*
  Selected by Mary Jo Bang

Landon Godfrey, *Inventory of Doubts*
  Selected by Dana Levin

Jesse Lee Kercheval, *America, that island
  off the coast of France* Selected by Ilya Kaminsky

Mario Chard, *Land of Fire*
  Selected by Robert Pinsky

Thomas Centollela, *Almost Human*
  Selected by Edward Hirsch

Lauren Camp, *One Hundred Hungers*
  Selected by David Wohjan

Maggie Smith, *The Well Speaks of Its
  Own Poison* Selected by Kimiko Hahn

Jeffrey Harrison, *Into Daylight*
  Selected by Thomas Sleigh

Ruth Ellen Kocher, *domina Un/Blued*
  Selected by Lynn Emanuel

Rusty Morrison, *After Urgency*
  Selected by Jane Hirschfield

Joshua Corey, *Severance Songs*
  Selected by Ilya Kaminsky

GC Waldrep, *Archicembolo*
  Selected by C.D. Wright

Sandra Meek, *Biogeography*
  Selected by Jeffrey Levine

David McCombs, *Dismal Rock*
  Selected by Linda Gregerson

Amaul Jamaul Johnson, *Red Summer*
  Selected by Carl Phillips

Rachel Contreni Flynn, *Ice, Mouth, Song*
  Selected by Stephen Dunn

Ilya Kaminsky, *Dancing in Odessa*
  Selected by Eleanor Wilner

It is quite commonplace when describing a new volume of poetry to resort to stock, albeit wholly appropriate, descriptors. "Stunning" and "dazzling" come immediately to mind. So, too, "compelling." I'm sure I've used such phrases myself, and would now when writing about *Asterism*, were this book not so fresh that it makes one self-conscious of, and encourages the reader to want to lean away from, anything resembling the familiar. The range in theme would be impressive enough on its own, but what sets this collection apart is how the author is able to pull off legitimate experimentation while remaining accessible. The poems both invite and challenge the reader. Here is a poet as intelligent as any other, but whose intelligence is never the point of the poem. Not to mention the language is downright gorgeous. Perhaps what is most striking about the collection is the apparent ease with which the author moves between registers and modes. At times personal, at others political; slipping back and forth between lyric and narrative; drawing on various languages and geographies, *Asterism* is a collection of both grace and grit, the work of a mind at work—in, and on, a world that is simultaneously expanding and contracting.   —*Dorset Prize judge John Murillo*

Born in South Korea and raised in Peru, AE HEE LEE is a migrant, scholar, translator, and poet currently living in Wisconsin. She is the author of *Asterism*, which won the 2022 Dorset Prize, and the poetry chapbooks: *Dear bear*, (Platypus Press 2021), *Bedtime || Riverbed* (Compound Press 2017), and *Connotary*, which was selected as the winner for the 2021 Frost Place Chapbook Competition. Her poetry has been published in *POETRY*, *The Georgia Review*, *New England Review*, and *Southern Review*, among others.

ASTERISM

Ae Hee Lee

T|P

TUPELO PRESS
North Adams, Massachusetts

ISBN-13: 978-1-961209-01-5 (paper)
Library of Congress Control Number: 2023945163

Text design by Howard Klein.

Cover art: Seongmin Ahn, "Portrait of Peony" Ink and color on mulberry paper, 2013. Copyright © Seongmin Ahn. Used by permission.

First paperback edition February 2024

Tupelo Press
P.O. Box 1767
North Adams, Massachusetts 01247
(413) 664-9611 / Fax: (413) 664-9711
editor@tupelopress.org / www.tupelopress.org

Tupelo Press is an award-winning independent literary press that publishes fine fiction, non-fiction, and poetry in books that are a joy to hold as well as read. Tupelo Press is a registered 501(c)(3) nonprofit organization, and we rely on public support to carry out our mission of publishing extraordinary work that may be outside the realm of the large commercial publishers. Financial donations are welcome and are tax deductible.

This project is supported in part by the National Endowment for the Arts

And everything conceals something else.
— *Italo Calvino*

Contents

*

Self-Portrait as Portrait   3

Inheritance :: Invocation   4

(Dis)ambiguation   6

Dream Series of my Mother Making Kimchi in Trujillo   7

Han-sum :: Breath, Singular   9

Self-Portrait as Mother   10

Self-Study through Daily Sustenance   11

Sijo :: Genealogy   16

**

Asterism   18

Trujillo :: Homecoming   20

Centers   21

Bongsung-a :: Impatient Balsam   22

(Dis)ambiguation   23

Chicago :: Re-entry Ritual   24

Prayer   25

Sijo :: Meeting Point   26

Upon Practicing a Second Language   27

Road Trip   28

El Milagro :: Edges   30

Anything You Can Find in the World You Can Find in the Body   32

Korea :: Things to Review Before Landing   35

Self-Study through Homes   36

Bougainvillea :: Papelillos   39

Home Remedies   40

Naturalization :: Migration   41

Self-Portrait as I   43

Mogyoktang :: Inside   44

On Borders   45

Midwest :: Equinox   46

Mending of Shoes   47

*
**

Green Card :: Evidence of Adequate Means of Financial Support   51

Papers   53

Madrugada :: Small Hours   54

When a Language is Said to be Lost   55

(Dis)ambiguation   56

Would I Rather Soften   57

La Esperanza :: Poinciana Tree   58

Grounding Exercise   59

Self-Study through Prefixes   60

Hyu :: In-Between   62

Conversation with Immigration Officer   63

Drinking Alone After the Rain Stops   67

Mercado Central :: Marginalia   68

Self-Portrait as Sister   70

Prelude   71

Notes   73

Acknowledgements   74

*

SELF-PORTRAIT AS PORTRAIT

Dearest you, I suspect
we were made tentatively: an exact

assemblage of organs, emotions—
complete with little
    phantom
pains.

       When your Korean was young, you asked
your father not to call you an *ingan*   *human*
because you didn't know
what the word meant
             but now

every day we meet at the edge
of every edge, our ankles
    frail for touching.

Together we are
         unhyphenated, indefinite, *country*
not *culture* not *skin*, clumsy
geese of three
wings: one for ourselves, one for the world,
               one for strangeness.

       Surely, some will continue to call us
inconvenient—

    we won't forget
    all beautiful things are.

INHERITANCE :: INVOCATION

    Because there's pleasure
in secrecy, I kneel in silence before
    a kitchen cabinet. I pull out
the large can of sesame oil
    inhabiting this corner of the house.
I remove the cap, bring my nose closer
    to the opening. The rim glistens
copper, the smell of an unfamiliar soil,
    a country I was born to but didn't
grow up with. I breathe it in. I breathe out:
    gosohada— this is still a word
I cannot translate until it evaporates.

*

    At times, my mother tells me about
my father, sets afloat hushed fairytales
    into the waters of my nights. She explains
my father is a lidded well: a closed circle
    of arms, thumb leaning on thumb,
how as the eighth son no one expected him
    to survive the winter. How he lives holding
a birth date that migrates with the moon.

*

    Can you love what you don't know?
I glance at the edge of a mirror,
    a crystal caught in my cornea. Maybe
the unknown is but a hard mirage of
    what's known, a questionable carbon copy
of the seer's mind. My curiosity draws me to this
    displaced image, selects from it;

my parents' nostalgia expands it, infinitely,
    like a prism. I want to love
what I don't know. I want to learn—
    allow myself this yearning.

*

    A homeland of mountains
with low, uneven shoulders.
    In the distance their outlines are
plumed as if made from torn paper.
    A homeland of electric forests,
persimmons, and expired peppermint
    candies in the shape of diamonds.
This land wasn't promised to me.
    But my memories open their palms.
They claim nothing as their own.
    They invoke. They let go.

*

    You have your father's face,
an aunt told me once. *A camel's long eyelashes*
    and dark stars for eyes. I admit my father has
passed onto me many of his idiosyncrasies:
    the closing of hands behind the back,
the bottling of desire until it bursts
    into a thousand iridescent needles of glass.
But when I visit his old house in Chungju,
    I don't call it home. I glimpse
a pair of cosmos flowers resting
    their heads against half-finished steps,
caress their purple ears and ask
    if they'll remember me from time to time.
I return to myself— broken and full.

(DIS)AMBIGUATION

All moons in all waters are that one moon
—Cho Oh-hyun

Before *immigrant*, noun
unproper, body of water
lusting after stars, prone
to flood, before *china!* and me
turning to look as if I was
referent, or even *ají*, Peruvian
pepper, affectionate nickname, *ajicita*—
and *unnie, unnie*, older sister, before
questioning a name, its relation
to skin, story, what's outside
but everything else,
before *alien*, untouchable
planet humming to be heard,
my parents spread open a hanja
dictionary on the hospital bed,
their fingertips lifted
a name from the paper:

사랑 :: 愛 :: heart cradled, carried slowly as cloud,
빛날 :: 熙 :: flower with a shining throat for lantern.

DREAM SERIES OF MY MOTHER MAKING KIMCHI IN TRUJILLO

I.

My mother and her wooden cooking spoon. A pot
filled with water and an ambiguous amount of all-purpose flour
instead of rice flour. She stirs. The water turns milky. It turns
thicker, stickier— the smell of starch dissipates into the air.
It occurs to me my mother's arm is an orbiting moon, unable to escape
the gravity of a planet much larger than itself.

                                                                    II.

                    My mother with salt on the flat of her hand, her arm extending
                         toward a ray of noon. She compares the Peruvian salt to another
                              memory. This unfamiliar salt in front of her eyes
                         is a thinner crystal. She licks her palm. It's slightly sour.
                              She asks me to come and have a taste, but I
                              have nothing to compare it with yet.

III.

My mother slicing onions, spring onions, radishes—
into whatever size she thinks would be "a pleasure to eat."
My mother's measuring tool: her intuition, her philosophy
that a fixation with authenticity deters one from pouring jeong
into the food. Jeong, she teaches me, is love
that comes with time, similar to the process of fermentation,
the slow dyeing of brined leaves.

My mother's concave back as she squats over the blue rim
of a plastic tub in the laundry room. The Napa cabbages inside are as wide
as my childish hips— rare in Trujillo, rare like the Korean pepper flakes
my mother has been saving by mixing them with ají panca. The translucent
plastic gloves covering her hands are smeared with bright candy red
and the green of spring onions. She tells me to go sleep first. I dream of her
hands carefully running between the cabbage leaves, even today,
half a continent away, making sure no white spot is left untouched.

HAN-SUM :: BREATH, SINGULAR

Literally, *han-sum* means the same
            strand of wind just unspooled
a little further.

                          *

    I sigh, and it's as if I've blown
onto my father's brow
until it crumples—

                          *

There's endlessness
in this word: an inward-
stretching universe of lungs
                    and dark matter.

                          *

At my sighing habit,
    my father rephrases
        an idiom, says, *at this rate*
    the draft will cleave
the ground under your feet,
        make the earth flicker
out like a sparkler's afterglow.

                          *

    His words assure me
even the smallest breath can
            ripple.

SELF-PORTRAIT AS MOTHER

After over twenty years in Peru, after burying
her father in Daegu, my mother visits me
in Wisconsin. We link arms (hers unbearably
light), walk down the Oak Leaf trail, glancing up
at the trees blanketed with silence, at the occasional
underbelly of bridges. She wants pictures.
With a shutter's click, I freeze the narrow creeks
by my mother's eyes. I notice her flourishing
pores, proof her face has been a kind host
to the dry Trujillan sky. As a little girl, I'd cup
her tears when she'd no one to talk to in Korean
about fruit vendors trying to scam her, mistaking her for a tourist
forever, taxi drivers asking her whether she was from China
or Japan, or another new acquaintance scolding,
This is how we do things here. Why wouldn't you
make things easier for yourself? Then I'd watch her move
past what others barely left ajar, insist on living
as a breathless field of seeds with its mouth always open.
She taught me how to be a foreigner,
garner my sunspots, some left by harsher stars,
some gentler, knit a plentiful basket out of myself.
Another day we'll rummage through it and relive ourselves
in each other. I show my mother the photo I've taken:
a lone piece of winter light had landed
on her left cheek, as if it too could sense in her
a glint of its future.

SELF-STUDY THROUGH DAILY SUSTENANCE

to eat
not only the skin, but the shade,
not only the sugar, but the days
—Li Young Lee

While in Michigan, I make it a habit to invite friends over for dinner. I enjoy experimenting with the miscellany of ingredients in the fridge. Measurements from this country still confuse me. But instead of forcing myself to translate kilos into pounds and vice versa, I choose to trust my hands, their memory of weight. My friends, one from Honduras, another from Guatemala and Korea, say my cooking reminds them of their homes somehow. Our hearts are their own stomachs; they fill with every spoonful we take.

*

For me, a sickly child, my mother prepares a warm bowl of congee, sprinkles it with shredded chicken and sesame seeds. From across the table, she watches me take one careful mouthful of soft rice at a time, barely restraining liquid snot with whatever strength I have left in my nostrils. My mother says she likes watching how each bite makes moons rise out of my eyes.

*

After a round of pulling at each other's hair for a trivial reason, I approach my sister with a split apple in hand— in Korean, the sound of the word *apple*, *sagwa*[1], also meaning *to ask for forgiveness*. We bite into the fruit and reconcile. I'm reminded forgiveness is something you can sink your teeth into, can limn what's sharp with honey.

---

[1] *Maracuyá.*   *Passion*
                fruit.   *Perilla.*
                        Kkaennip.   Lúcuma.
                                                                                    See
        how   they   wreathe
                                                my tongue,
                        how their sounds
                                                        wet   my mouth
    with hunger.

*

This is the first time I'm on my own. My family and friends in a different hemisphere. Home-sickness is a woman with a blurry face who wears my mother's worn apron, beckons me to cook what I cannot easily find near me. I fill the pot with broth, and she licks the spoon. *What's missing?* I ask daily. She says, *Maybe a dash of soy sauce, or some crushed garlic cloves, two of those little bulbous teeth, for depth.* On a different day, she instructs, *Rub the oregano between your fingers to wake its scent.* Or, *For the rice, place your hand on top, pour the water in until it makes an archipelago out of your knuckles.* I try to find my way back home through the kitchen, but she scolds, *Consider the potatoes: a yukon gold is a yukon gold, not a papa yungay.* I move on to broil something new.

*

My grandmother takes me to Gyeongju to see the old Korean temples and palaces. On the road we meet a field of pink-winged lotuses and leaf pads colored somewhere between blue and green, so large girls could be boated in them.

Later, their roots[2], nursed unseen under beds of loam, appear on my plate, each thin slice carved with the flower they bore, braised in sweet soy.

*

Five years in Peru was what it took for my father's stomach to cease understanding the spicy love language of Korean red peppers. Now, when he cooks instant ramen, he makes sure to pinch out the crimson flakes mingling in the dehydrated forest of green onions and mushrooms.

Two in the U.S. and I get heartburn from licking clean the lime milk from a ceviche platter.

---

[2] If I'm
        what I eat, then let me
chew
    on root,   become something
                like possibility.

*

A classmate comes over to my house for a school project. She asks for a glass of milk and follows me into the kitchen. As soon as I open the fridge, she pinches her nose; the sharp smell of freshly fermented kimchi greets us both. I want to say something about history and culture, recite a long list of health benefits, the hours my mother toiled to make this dish— but a glance at her grimace and a senseless sense of shame bewilder me into silence, and shame me twice.

*

At the outskirts of Trujillo, a church with a guinea pig[3] pen in the back. I'm a child who slips in to play with the little creatures, bribe them with alfalfa stalks for their friendship. One day, an hermana comes and swoops up a group of them. I follow her into the kitchen, where she picks one up, twists its neck with the might of her motherly arm; the tiny bones pop with the sound of bottle caps. I can't move. She bathes the guinea pig in boiling water, a blistering baptism, undresses it expertly from the tricolored fur I had petted just minutes ago. Its bare skin so much like mine, pinkish and veined. The hermana proceeds to remove the insides, brine the frame, embalm it with oil and cumin. The fire licks its lips over the coals until it is given the fatty meat to grill. A small beast growls inside my stomach. The people gather. Together we pray and break into the animal's body.

*

For Alejandra, food is an infiltrator. My childhood friend tells me about a boy she loved, how he once cooked pasta for her while the sound of light rain painted the background. The boy moved to another city, but she tells me she is like a leaf, who drank deep only to realize her fate had irrevocably joined the water's. Both the boy and the rain remain in her body still, seeping.

3

                      The plate mirrors
                            the earth
we glean,
so to devour must be
     to live
               in karma.

*

A red flower, which my memory has turned anonymous. When it blooms, its petals don't widen. They gather and bow as one, allowing only its pistil, yellow with pollen and sun, to loll out. I'm five, and a girl from France transfers into my school. She likes to pluck the flower, leave its sepal intact, and suck the bottom for nectar. A girl with a red flower for lips. I'm twenty-five, and sometimes I think of her. I wonder if she still collects sweet things under her hummingbird tongue.

*

For a late-night snack, I want to nibble on something ancient. I go out to the streets looking for anticuchos: pieces of cow heart staked on a sugarcane stick, dipped in flame, crowned with a boiled sweet potato. They say marinating the organ in ají panca and herbs was the idea of the Incas. The skewers, of the Spanish. I bite. I taste the savory meat melded with violence. I swallow and survive another day.

*

A gift of a dozen blue eggs. My father cracks one over the pan and provokes its yolk with a fork. *Come and see—it doesn't tear.* I mutter a prayer: may my life be as tenacious.[4]

*

In fairy tales and myths, people are warned not to eat from the strange place they've lost themselves in, or they won't be able to leave it. Persephone swallows six pomegranate seeds

---

[4]   In the end, the things I crave are

        those that can't live

             forever.   An avocado that bruises,

                                  soft,   soft

                                         with flavor.

from the underworld and becomes wedded to Hades forever. In each country I call home, I eat my way into belonging.[5]

*

Parents believe that if you make children plant their own vegetables, it's more likely they will eat them. And yet I water my garden of beets with a delicate undulation of wrist and hose but will not welcome them into my mouth. A beet snaps upon harvest and the color of its meat clings onto my palm, crimson, as if to say, *Look, in loneliness we are all the same.*

*

Every Christmas season in Peru, a box of Panetón. Bell-shaped loaf wrapped in wax paper woven with star polyhedrons, sweet and airy bread laced with fruit jelly, golden tufts we pull apart and slather with butter— a tradition my Korean family gladly takes under their tongues.

Years later, in an aisle of an Italian market in Milwaukee, I catch the sight of a box that reads, "Panettone." It suddenly strikes me Italian immigrants had baked them first into South American countries. All along, I'd been taking into my body centuries of trails, nourishing myself, perhaps into a morsel for someone else's future.

*

My mother teaches me that in Korean to forget is also expressed as *to have peeled,* like you would an unsuspecting mango, *and eaten away a memory.* When I tell her I'm afraid of forgetting things— the cottony texture of guaba seeds, the freckles of the faces I've loved— she reminds me I may eat and forget, forget and eat, but the soul grows all the same, a little fuller each time.

5

                                               So often   my longing

                             for a kinder world

has been a scalded
palate, going for
                 another
                     spoonful of soup   that won't cool.   And yet—

SIJO :: GENEALOGY

My father liked to tease with an old pun,
           saying he found me
under the *dari*, the arch
           of my mother's *dari*, her splayed legs—
I felt fortunate to be called
           the daughter of a bridge.

**

ASTERISM

It's true: today too

the sky arches

in faithful trajectory and

even when there's no eye

to keep it company, it unfurls

stars for the season.

Tonight, I pray for wonder,

innocent thread

without a needle, to play-

pretend embroidering

the missing

links between a satellite's

silver, the dying

borders of a sore,

an oxtail bone

I once nibbled clean,

my grandmother's braids

turned tinsel after two wars,

words, *aluminum, allure,*

alumbrar, aludir— Because

I hear yesterday's

cloud might shed

rain over some stranger

I'll meet another day

and the sheen over red

pomegranate seeds

on my sister's hand warbles

white like the sea

connecting us. I confess

I have many questions,

but I leave them

unresolved for tomorrow

and tomorrow: every luminous

body: periphery and center,

part lyre, part storied lover,

not a single one untethered.

TRUJILLO :: HOMECOMING

Alejandra welcomes me back
to our first home, her arms
wide ferns, her fingers wispy
fronds curling towards
me, towards a small sun
blushing on my cheek. She puckers
her lips to greet the wind
which sings secretly, close to my ear—
Alejandra welcomes me back
and my heart stutters. I don't
remember whether to turn my face left
or right. I whisper, *it's okay,*
es normal— for there to be sorrow
in forgetting how to cross
through gaps, now filled
with the gossamers of time.
Gwaenchanh-a, está bien—
for people to become strangers
to their own bodies, question
why absences insist on being
woven into something new.
Alejandra welcomes me back,
so I go— receive her beso:
I too unfurl green, under
the embrace of lush
unfamiliar arms.

CENTERS

In Peru, when I was asked if Korea was inside the U.S,
a centavo fell off my wallet and rolled under the vending machine. I sticked
my fingers into the dusty gap, but the coin was lost, no doubt,
though only to me.

In Korea, I was asked if Peru was inside the U.S.
It was cold, and winter had no need of me, but I was still
there, doing no more than a grain of salt,
warming the asphalt street.

In the U.S.: where was Korea, where was Peru.
I replied every time by looking at my belly button, narrating
the long string of belly buttons that came before it.

BONGSUNG-A :: IMPATIENT BALSAM

Monsoon in Busan, garden balsams
plump with rain. My cousin and I gather them greedily,
and we arrive to her house, our arms fragrant and shining.
She crushes the flowers, whole with silky stem, and we take
turns wrapping the paste around the curve of our fingers.
The weight of moist petals presses against our virgin nailbeds,
stains the plates a glistening orange-red. I search for meaning
in everything, and here: the belief in true love
if the color lasts until first snow.

Lake Michigan at the coda of a polar vortex. At the edge,
I can't distinguish snow from foam, but I'm sure the ice would
taste sweet with its coral glow. My cuticles flake under the gloves—
my nails thirst. I think of all the promises that have yet
to be made. I remain a stranger to many myths, but not this.

(DIS)AMBIGUATION

Occasionally an automated e-mail
or a person I just met halves my name,
addresses me as *Dear Ae,*
not knowing this
to also mean *Dear Love,*

*

Are these the names they call themselves too,
I wonder: *Sparrowhawk— Bluethroat—*
Many times, I've not recognized
myself— a fistful of dark feathers
caught between a caller's teeth.

*

At a coffee shop, I introduce myself as *Ruth.*
The cashier scribbles it down on the cup,
says, *What an American name!*
about the woman
who had become a foreigner
for a foreigner.

CHICAGO :: RE-ENTRY RITUAL

I've become an expert
    at packing exactly 50 lbs.
worth of breadcrumbs.
    The luggage: the head
I unload mid-flight. I leave
    a snowy trail over the Pacific.
The fish swallow my way back,
    but I know the tale
will remain. Upon landing,
    I look back; my eyes crust
with salt. I wander through
    the labyrinth of customs,
praying for safe passage
    in a mixed tongue.
What's the purpose of your visit?
    they ask. *What's the purpose of me?*
I ask and answer myself every time:
    to be reunited with love, waiting
at every side of a border,
    to consider a country isn't a womb
though a womb can be a country,
    to carry the migrant dust
on my limbs, the remnant
    skin cells from people
who embraced me goodbye,
    to let them weigh my hems,
to die like a candle to a kiss
    at each point of entry—rename
my departures into returns.

PRAYER

Where does an echo start
when the mouth is also eco?

How to praise
the tongue warming the body,

how it's infinite
in its brokenness.

When I sought for cordilleras,
I found moths and bone

mountains, language
loitering like a mul-gwishin:

ghost of thick eyelashes
dripping with bitter honey.

Lord, she pulls me
daily into emerald

lagunas. If I follow her
until the end, will she transmute

my voice into a lacunae
unhushed?

SIJO :: MEETING POINT

Wisconsin's sky this evening is a glass
                half-full of storm clouds.
For a second, they are also mountains, lilac,
                haloing the rooftops of Cajamarca.
But I'm not there
          nor now.

UPON PRACTICING A SECOND LANGUAGE

I understood speech as a manner of wind.
Voice could be voiceless, place nestled inside palate,
the dark side of teeth or a throat's deep.
When I couldn't parse *oo* from *root* and *foot*,
ears and letters showed themselves dragonflies
lured young by the smell of sap, hardened within
splintering amber. In the end, I chose to laugh
when I repeated

> *desért*

désert

> > *dessért*

driven mad with intention, until I found out
what word I truly craved. Like this,
I dropped my words into wishing wells;
not believing it a waste.
Some days I noticed that to delight in the whimsy
of meaning could also be a sign I was lonely, wanting
to be, wanting to long— but I was happy too.
I could savor the second a violet
turned violent in my radiant mouth.

ROAD TRIP

Our hands loll out the car windows,
      Tal vez solo yo lleno
Hola, hola—to bewilder the corn stalks
      Esta canción de recuerdos ajenos
on our way to Chicago. Morning
      Temiendo perder
hasn't widened yet into afternoon,
      Contra lo que se pierde
but a September moon is out early to overhear us
      La tristeza que le sigue
sing Bacilos' "Caraluna" in unison.
      Poco a poco esta sencillez de sentimientos
The rearview mirror diligently catches
      Estoy segura de que desvanecerán
our miles, which seem to roll away
      Así como todo cuerpo
like apples, but the road reappears
      Toda pena
before us anew as a yet untroubled sheet
      Hasta este camino de riachuelo y cielo
of water. Steadily or not, we move forward
      Pero al menos en este momento
while looking back: the three of us,
      Pido por algo más profundo
each from a different Latin American town,
      Aún más absoluto
how we tangled our bodies toward the music,
      Que la pérdida y el olvido
behind our Korean parents' backs,
      No desconoceré que los días son cortos
as our first loves spun us around senseless
      Y sé que de hecho diremos adiós

under blushing magenta lights,
>
> *Más veces que las semillas de girasol*

how we're meant for beautiful
>
> *Pero por ahora cantamos*

meetings, how history is also made of these.
>
> *Estamos aquí*

In the middle of a highway
>
> *Estamos aquí*

that's not ours, our voices,
>
> *Y la luna nos seguirá*

like tin bells, ache to shatter
>
> *Hasta el fin de la pista*

this song we share
>
> *Cantando también*

against the wind.
>
> *Bella, desafinada*

EL MILAGRO :: EDGES

"This is what the sun would taste like
if stored in a fridge," Alejandra says,

as she hands me a perfectly round
slice of pineapple, chilled,
half-dressed in a thin plastic bag.

She smiles, her face casting
an umbra, in which I am

a visitor.
Once I read each heart knows
its own bitterness,

and no one else
can share its joy. But we sit, our backs

mothered by this wall.
We: a brief intersection
of elbows, a small choir of helpless slurps—

our mouths flooding and the juice
dripping freely, dribbling down

the length of our tanned fingers,
down to dot
the sand until we reach

the middle—tough
to the touch of our teeth.

I mistake it for seed, but it's not

seed. It's corazón, coeur,
a core—

what brings together
a fruit's flesh.

She eats until her hands empty,
while I can't. It's hard
and not so sweet.

ANYTHING YOU CAN FIND IN THE WORLD YOU CAN FIND IN THE BODY

I. *In Trujill*o

> a man crouches
> with a knife
> buried under his ribs

i'm eleven and within the gash
i see glistening crimson
pearls   strawberry candies removed

> from a mouth's viscous enclosure
> sugar surrendering
> its syrup to the sun witnessing

> a pair of brown legs running
> away   slowly
> soaking with gravity   while

> somewhere   rain muddies the ground
> an unending velvet handkerchief
> from a magic show

flutters   because it could disappear
at any moment   the squeals
of children playing tag

> hands   cold   seeking
> sanctuary in a lover's pocket
> an entire ocean   ebbing red

> with relentless dusk

II. *In Milwaukee*

i leave
     a TV blinking
          with the news   another shooting

          as if picking up
               where it left off   the world continues
  to spill out

     from the most recent body's side
older now   i know how to be
          afraid   get angry at the trade: metal

for possibility   get chrysanthemums
          and watch them wither
i keep trying

          to turn my mourning into
                    something
                    meaningful

though the body bleeding out
     today is the body
          bleeding

               out tomorrow
          and hope   feels more
like suffering

          to not become the doe
which stays frozen   in place
          replacing its fear

with angels
mesmerized by the bright
            headlights   descending

to crush it

KOREA :: THINGS TO REVIEW BEFORE LANDING

My origin story:

My mother found me as a chestnut dangling from a
tree. When I fell onto her lap, she was eating
a copper pear with one hand, paging through
a book with the other. She carried out the burr
in the hollow of her arms; the spiny cupule made her
bleed, but she didn't surrender me until I dropped
from the shell. Later, I sprouted needles anew, afraid
I was being nibbled away by the world.

My grandfather's name:

I thought my grandfather's name was Hal-abeoji,
only to find out it was the Korean word for
grandfather. He was the one who taught me and my
sister to sail a paper kite over a frozen river, to allow
my index to flirt with its mercurial tail.

An idiom:

When I was given a norigae to hang
under my first hanbok jacket, I foresaw
a pendulous love in my life. I alternated
between laughing and sobbing. Short horns
appeared on my back. From then on, a child-like
misfortune took the shape of a blank page and
muffled my steps in every new country I called
home. I didn't want her at first, but eventually grew
fond of her, held her hand when she cried at night.

A road:

The one I took to school when I lived in Jang-yu
for that one year. I studied the occasional
bush of forsythias on the side prodding yellow against
an absolute autumn sky.

SELF-STUDY THROUGH HOMES

We live in imaginary countries
—Etel Adnan

When people ask where I'm from, where I'm *really* from, I ready my permutations. My mélange of autumnal streets, my obscure cities, the countries I found constructed on a mound of papers and tears, the pebble-sized universe occupying my left shoe— I want to tell them everything. I want to see how far we can go.

*

A Venezuelan couple moves into our neighborhood. They share their story with me, why they migrated to Peru: the inflation, the hunger and fear, their love— They're relieved they can send money back to their families. They say they miss the soup their grandmother used to make, the sleepiness after eating it, the magic. When I ask what's home for them, they say home is a fist that dreams.

*

Instead of calling home by the name of a country, I imagine calling it by people's names or pronouns. *Hello, I'm from Sang-Hee. I'm going back to Alejandra. Have you ever visited Daniel? I'm proud of you. I miss me.*

*

I realize I've been acquainted with my husband for less time than I have my parents, who received and kept my first laughter like a pressed flower in the folds of their memory. Less time than my sister, who would only fall asleep when my hair was twined around her thumb, an amulet against nightmares. I didn't expect I would end up staying in the States after finishing my studies; I find it strange I fell in love with a stranger. Though maybe it was because he was a stranger, and it's easier for me to love strangers. One day, the years I've known him will claim half my life, then maybe most of it, but never all. This, the life of an immigrant too.

*

I ask my parents whether they miss Korea. My father crosses his arms. Says home is now. My mother, next to him, adds home is also then.

*

A documentary explains how at one point, a hermit crab must seek for a new home, a new shell to protect its curved abdomen, pliant as grape, easy cooking target for the sun. It'll meet others by the shore, where they'll line up patiently from largest to smallest, swap shells that match their present size. A systematic method of survival that benefits everyone— except for the one left out. It sears into my mind. Not the idea of one being left out but the image of the crab, its toy-orange legs flailing, hurrying after a shell with a hole on its roof that will just have to do for an uncertain while.

*

I ask a friend whose life oscillated between Trujillo and Lima, where's home for her these days. She says home is any place that calls her name.

*

At the airport, the day I would stop sharing a roof with my family, my mother tucks the word *Saranghae* deep into the pocket of my ear. She repeats, *Saranghae, Saranghae, Saranghae—* until the word I'd heard everyday sounds like a foreign language, until the word sheds the husk of its meaning and is replaced with music.

*

There was a time I thought home was a pair of hand-me-down pants I'd eventually grow into. But home was the blur of my body, in which the same bloodstream didn't flow twice, in which a deep breath let my lungs embrace my heart tighter, before letting go.

*

In my mailbox: a welcome letter and a 3x2 inch card. It declares I've been granted temporary permission, acceptance, to be where I already am. I could drill a hole in it with my stare: this small key on the palm of my hand, green like a pair of emerald earrings I never had, the application fees that continue to increase like an insidious night of bloating grass, thought harmless by those who don't dream of it without realizing it's not a dream. Green, the color of my conditional privilege, my temporary relief, built upon others' anxieties. All condensed into a single object I'm asked to carry at all times but made so easy to lose, so I could, easily, lose my place here.

*

I'm tired. I read about how policies attempting to restrict migration constantly fail, unable to forbid the body, the cities and deserts it carries inside, the winds wrinkling its lakes, the finches darting not only above but under its airport ceilings. I'm tired, so I lay down. The earth spins for me and the dead continue their orbiting. It gives me strength: to remember there is no such thing as an immovable object.

BOUGAINVILLEA :: PAPELILLOS

Alejandra says she doesn't believe in discovery,
only in encounters, and that she wants to introduce me
to a bougainvillea bush down the street. She leads us
past white window gates from colonial times
that look like ornate birdcages, and I don't ask out loud
whether a single dust particle has remained
in place since I left Trujillo years ago. She points, smiling,
Look, the branches of papelillos are over there— hugging
the sky. They are the color of our mornings here, of light
shivering in fog, busy with petals that are not petals but
leaves holding invisible flowers. We don't stand too close;
we don't interrupt the rustle of paper chalices
above our heads. We wait under the latticed shade, stay
still to understand what it means to sway.

HOME REMEDIES

For bee stings, my parents would rub a spoonful of doenjang on my skin until it scabbed. For burns, they wrung the aloe vera in our backyard for its tears. For scraped knees, a song: *Sana, sana colita de rana, si no sanas hoy, sanarás mañana*—promised me all tadpole tails grew back, eventually. For homesickness, I crooned the same song. It didn't work. I found out then the ability to heal diminishes with age. But it mattered little.

I sang. I sang anyway.

NATURALIZATION :: MIGRATION

At a pottery sale,
I buy nothing, only
            consider this

    turquoise-ribbed vase, baked
    into a gloss of rivers,
slightly slanted to the left.

So, so cheap— perhaps
a uniqueness mistaken
            for a mistake.

I'm convinced
    of its fragility,
            its ceramic pelvis.

        The space
        . it would take up
    in the immigration bag

    my parents passed down
to me: dark, foldable closet
            I've dragged

from country to country.
When I was younger,
        I orphaned many books;

now I just carry
this guilt,
    a jealousy

for roots, a garland
of delicate hair seeping
        slowly into soil—

into vase.
        But I'm no perennial
        green. I have feet

eager to get naked,
        moved by the seasons
not here yet.

                        They ask me to chase
        their undulating
animal dreams.

SELF-PORTRAIT AS I

I think, therefore I am. Or am I
lying here because you think of me:
your back blooms: my spine, a caterpillar,
has found a resting place on it: you a warm
line adding to my line: we converge
into a single letter, write out the hanja 人
over the swirling galaxy
of our dark blankets to mean us a soul.
In Spanish, *yo* is the first person singular,
a pair made from consonant and vowel. With my air
and your ear, we utter into existence.
And *I* stands alone, until
we get intimate, peel the dress from its diphthong
thighs. *Ai*: love, morning and you rise
for me. Ready the scent of eggs and coffee.
Our *yo* omitted, personhood and time
infused into action. Outside:
the city stirs to make the city.

MOGYOKTANG :: INSIDE

From the entrance, the steam smells of pine leaf
and boiled eggs— I sink

into one of the hot tubs, quickly become raw skin,
conditioned timidity I can't reason away, mauve heat

blush with a nervous eye on a towel, which had assured me
it would conceal the soft folds of my stomach. I'm not

alone. There are others more accustomed to bareness,
close by. Today, we all wear the same teal

waters, every quivering droplet: together
we tread the tiled floor as moons

of milk fat, of dark budding nipples and creviced
thighs, of wide stony hips, of tender

skin, exfoliated from mineral sweat and grime— and I, pulse
and curve, feel lightheaded in the

warm water, or the beauty of something so ordinary
like the body. Inside this mogyoktang, I start to believe

I can hide away from eyes and words
that hunger. I lean back, drift

into a time long before shame
was something to dress for.

ON BORDERS

I.

I carry a piece of chalk around,
gift ribs to empty sidewalks. I draw
my lines with ease.

II.

Under a eucalyptus tree,
I stretch my fingers, just beyond
the boundary of shade, venture
under the light's fair blade.
I marvel at how a body can inhabit
worlds at a time.

III.

I ask a map why does an oasis
stops extending its waters
where it does. And it asks
how far would I go for an eye
clasping a feral dawn, teeming
with a thousand weary evenings.

IV.

I overhear a man talk about this country
as if it were a walnut splitting under
the pressure of desire. I recognize
the crack threading the husk—a hole
forfeiting its seed to a chamber
full of teeth. I walk over and say
a country is not a walnut. He says it is
his walnut, and bites down.

MIDWEST :: EQUINOX

For most of my life, I slept
by the music of sand dunes
shifting yearlong. But today
I wake up, spot a snowflake
melting into the window's glass.
I think I'll never grasp the true
width of the world. Because even this
land is a trickster, bidding
the ivory humps of winter
leviathans to thaw
into strings of water, scurry
and make a sea out of a sloping garden.
I hurry outside. I witness the way
a warm whisper rouses children
of tiny green fingers.

MENDING OF SHOES

It's said that by gifting
shoes to your loved ones
you risk them
leaving you.

*

Yet, my father
suggests I should try
on the ones in the shop
window, fully
in the knowledge
they'll spirit me away.

*

The shoes are tanned
leather, the color of quail.
They hold me up
like bones.

*

They carry me
to Michigan, along
the lake, in search of bus stops
through snow, coasting
highways; they stop
at the occasional orange
lamplight suspended
in an alien darkness.

*

They collapse
gradually, steadily
at the heels.
Both of their toe tips
bruise with salt.

*

Once the strings
finish fraying, they gape
like lilies, tired
from completing
a blossoming.

*

It's summer.
We go back to Trujillo,
where a desert's winter
begins to whistle.

*

My mother takes us
to the cobbler
by the church of San Agustín.
She haggles, while I keep
the shoes tucked under
my arms, covering their eyes
as if they were a small animal.

*

In the airport once again,
caught in a layover. My eyes
fall upon the new soles,
stamped with a brand
I don't recognize.
The leather has been painted
over, but some scratches
remain for good.

*

For this, which warms
my feet, for every senseless
reason considered
enough, gratitude knots
my heart tighter.

*

Around me, crowded
steps land on polished floor,
sounding a mess
of colorful pearls, spinning
off into all directions.

✱✱

GREEN CARD :: EVIDENCE OF ADEQUATE MEANS OF FINANCIAL SUPPORT

I needed money. There's no poetic way to say this.
Even so, when you touched my face, brought my
cheeks to the nook of your neck, I burrowed into it—
a firefly seeking shelter from winter, far
underground. Then,

> you told me there's no application form that can hold
> the entirety of a life, because our days constantly spill like wine.
> *Imagine that*, you said, *apricot tones all over the page!*

> you told me about ferns, bejeweled with jade dew,
> their coiled fiddleheads full of unfulfilled,
> twirling futures, and I forgot about my fixation with earning
> people's respect, among other things for which
> I'd been told it was proper to plead
> until granted.

> you told me, if immigrants could enrich a country,
> you didn't want to know
> our melting point and whether we would shine
> brighter than gold.

> you told me how I could stop confusing *belonging*
> with *belongings*, *good* with *goods*, by sharing
> the way our hearts continue to beat
> resilient, even without an assurance of worth.

> you told me there can be solace in a dead end, in knowing the sea
> still collapses, still runs and soars carrying its broken
> shells, somewhere out there. Then,

you buried a kiss in the dark
earth of my hair. I believed it all.
What else could I do?

PAPERS

At the office, I hear the crinkling ghosts of leaves.
Trees don't exist in this space. Eucalyptus, aspen, nor birch.
There's paper, skinny knives and fine print.
There's no blood in this place, nothing
which oozes, may smear. On my lap,
I have my paperwork for a social security number.
I think I can hear some sighs, outside, thumping
their wispy heads against the wall
next to me. I think how the difference
between me and those who aren't here happens
to be paper-thin—

I continue to wait for my turn. I begin to fold
a crane. I sculpt wings
for remembrance (of what doesn't exist),
a tiny and pointy beak as strong as
an old wives' tale. I crease a wish inside,
leaning in with the ballpoints of my fingers
(which don't exist). I'm so busy
I almost miss my turn.

MADRUGADA :: SMALL HOURS

6:03 a.m. and unripe sunlight percolates through air, canopy of oak, window and yellow
curtain, into my living room. It must have been a day like this:

The birth of a word.

The word an offering,
      hatching within a fertile mind.

The instance a small god
      many have beheld at least once:

           a large jellyfish with the body of an unraveling clementine, passing through—

The house billows. Luminous cells skip across the walls, and even the grey couch gleams,
flecks of morning made crescent with the shadow of leaf.

WHEN A LANGUAGE IS SAID TO BE LOST

or prodigal, it's really underway.
This is the principle of mass conservation:
that memory can be exhausted into feathery grey
ashes, but the mind, like hair, can't help but absorb,
carry the smell of smoke wherever it goes. Belonging
splits easier than an atom into *being, longing*, and language, yes,
I have known it to erode into dust, but also birth
a new mountain within the mouth.

(DIS)AMBIGUATION

America, I hear, as in *American, American dream.*
   America— and a portion of the continent vanishes.

America: the name slips out my mouth
   like a sticky cherry pit. *America*, I say again,

and this time I feel as if I've plucked
   a geranium from Alejandra's eyes,

the park in Trujillo, where we used to play hide-and-seek.
   Years ago, I learned *America* was a word coined

centuries earlier by someone not from *America*,
   after an Italian explorer who circled

the shadows of *America*'s earthen body, the earliest use
   of *America* being almost ten thousand years after

la papa—the potato—was replanted
   over and over and weaned off its venom

by hands often made invisible by *America*.
   Please, I can't say *America* without noticing

its first button is in the wrong hole.

WOULD I RATHER SOFTEN

The way a cup of black tea is easily changed
by milk or light—
The way soybeans are left to soak
until they bloat. Blended until they are broken
down into paste and pressed into a brittle clump of tofu—
The way a drumstick is forgotten at the back of the fridge,
and months turn muscle into a fuzzy forest of mold—
You can't choose when
grief will knead your heart sore.
But as a child, when I asked my mother why the pill bug
rolled into a solitary planet when it was afraid,
she suggested we practice softness—
listen to what it had to say.
And this too didn't leave us unscathed.

LA ESPERANZA :: POINCIANA TREE

In La Esperanza, stands a barren poinciana tree.
We climb over it, scratching its callused bark
with our sandals. Breathless, our faces
are like berries, petite and round
flames. We place airy leaflets behind our ears
and chuckle. The neighbor doesn't like us
on the tree, which extends its branches
towards her eaves, and so one day,
we come back to a nest of barbed wires
scrawled on the treetop. *How sad...*
We say to no one in particular.
How pitiful, our poinciana tree...
With the belief it would rather be
hurt by us, we leave it
to play house in a different garden.

GROUNDING EXERCISE

When i'
m hovering
over the country i'
m in, when i
don't feel held, i
hold a thing. i
notice the wooden
torso of a pencil
under my
thumb, the thin
layer of yellow
paint, the dints—
it's warm (or is that
me?). i
leave the room,
go outside,
come down
to the soil, dig a little,
and loosen the dirt. i
see what makes the weed
persist: a
grave of broken
roots, cities
run by worms,
the secret
bones of a mammoth,
fallen things
which
haven't failed.

SELF-STUDY THROUGH PREFIXES

Multi-: more than one; many, especially variegated. Example: "multicolor." Think kaleidoscope. A spinning circus of several colored-glass. From the Latin *multus*, "much, many." The existence of more than one. In one. Example: "multicultural." Think you. Think of those you love. Think myriads of others: strangers you could love.

*

Notice people applaud at the word "unity." And yet, words like "mixture," "composite," and "amalgamation" are often attributed to Frankenstein's creature. Abomination. The "monster" (from the Latin *monere* or warn) must be hidden, devoured, or assimilated (notice though, "monster" sounds closer to the Latin *monstrare* which means "to show"). Notice you are not alone in your desire for this being to have a name of its own.

*

Another prefix: *inter-*. From the Old French *entre-* or Latin *inter-*. Between, among. Poet Kimberly Blaeser once talked about a liminal space in which mixed bloods and mixed cultures find themselves. She called the in-between not a phase of being but a state of being, not a tragedy but a position of power. A strength and balance that only bridges possess. Don't forget "Intermediary"— don't underestimate it.

*

Read Andersen's "The Little Mermaid," again. The ending: the little mermaid cannot go back to be a mermaid, having been human, and cannot become human, having been mermaid. Her sisters at the sea, the prince for whom she endured the pain of invisible knives needling her soles— neither understood her love. When she turns into foam, don't cry for her, don't hate the story. Read it again.

*

Prefix: *cross-* Surprise: originating from the word "cross." Can refer to the shape of a cross, or across. Example: "Crossroads": An intersection of two or more roads. Neither here nor there. Figuratively, a meeting place. A shared place, a place of sharing, which belongs to no one for those that belong nowhere. Old European folklore tells stories of fairy processions happening at crossroads. A threshold to new worlds.

*

Recall the Venn diagram from your math class: a diagram of logical relations between different sets. The more circles, the closer to a field of flowers. Admire Venn diagrams, watch how the circles always converge in the middle. Ask: who fits outside these spaces of meeting? Who can live untouched and alone?

*

Another prefix that means across: *trans-*. Also means beyond and through. In *Third Factory*, Viktor Shklovsky writes, "There is no third alternative. Yet that is precisely the one that must be chosen." To transform oneself is to transcend. An unchanging thing is a dead thing.

*

Learn from words. Words know that they cannot be restricted to a single meaning, and that their many meanings become their history and identity. Learn from people: words come from people—they were made in their image.

*

In his essay "The Argentine Writer and Tradition" Borges thought there were no camels in the Koran and wrote that "[Mohammed] knew he could be Arab without camels." Wonder: what do you not need, to be what you are?

HYU :: IN-BETWEEN

At all sides, the trains slip away from us.
    My sister and I play Red light, Green light

but with eyes closed and singing instead:
    the-hi-bis-cus-sy-ria-cus-has-bloomed-a-gain!

Our mother glances at the platform clock
    and us, as we practice the art of climbing stairs

slowly, anoint each step with the shadows of scissors, wolves,
    shapeshifters we call hands. It's a quiet

and passionate affair— to dwell
    in the meanwhile, with a waiting so bright

red like the beads of jujube fruits
    our grandmother used to dry

out in the yard, so they would amass all
    the sweetness of the world in their little bodies.

She taught me nothing is wasted
    in waiting, and to be grateful for the sun,

which won't ever hurry. Years after, she's no longer with us.
    I hum: *mu-gung-hwa-kkoch-i-pieo-sseub-ni-da!*

And a train nuzzles the station,
    as it arrives, arrives, and arrives.

CONVERSATION WITH IMMIGRATION OFFICER

She looks at your papers.
She asks your husband to step out.
She asks you where your husband's birthplace is.
She is testing you. You answer:

we were made in water in free-flowing

salt water rich with plankton

& we keep a fire

in our lungs it burns white

red in the center like a hibiscus

you must know we are all manic

you must know we are not ink

more than pencil-point residue

graphite ...

She asks for the address of your current home.
You clear your throat and fold your hands on your lap.
Secretly, you imagine you have just met her
in a train, on the way to some undecidedly lovely place.

we are living

in this continent for now

we had to leave paradise

when we became of age a common ritual

how about you? did you know

this continent is but a well-rooted boat?

did you know roots are easy

to snap?

The officer has a catalog of potential questions in her eyes.
You are the last question mark inside that list.
She asks if you have committed any crimes.

i have lied before

my memories

& my world are

being devoured

by bright lime groves

but i am committed to lie

with love

to live

i thought everyone

committed lies

& wants

She asks what you had for breakfast.
What your husband had for breakfast.
You smile at what could have been
a question asked by a friend.

i pressed pearly remains

of snow into my mouth

drop drop drop ...

i didn't share

he peeled & ate a secret

he didn't share

either

But the officer doesn't smile back.
She asks if you understand what she is saying.

i don't dream in languages

only in prophecies

& whale songs

Your lawyer, sitting behind you,
says everything is going to be all right.

i believe stories

become real

when you ache

yes, yes, don't words make you want

to believe?

But she isn't smiling either. You shiver.
The air conditioner is always too cold, too powerful
in this country.

see how inside my thorax

minute icicles

prickle and shake

slightly at each hiccup

    no ... yes ... no ...

The officer says you will hear from them
in a couple of months. She asks you to leave.
She asks your husband to step in.

        yes ...

DRINKING ALONE AFTER THE RAIN STOPS

After Li Bai

Petrichor's in the air, scent of wet soil
fading. I take out the makgeolli from the fridge.
A migratory cloud perches on my cup of rice wine,
takes flight as soon as I part my lips.
Gentle alcohol in my mouth's
ribbed cathedral. Down the throat,
and I drown for a second. The world
waves— liquid silk drifts along
my blood. The body is a good vessel,
I can tell. So well-versed in relinquishing.
But why do I thirst daily to say, *I have*—
love, a country, history— things
born from togetherness that pour out
like the rainclouds that come and go, this drink
I share with what's left of the day.

MERCADO CENTRAL :: MARGINALIA

Out
of the corner of my eye: a man
pushing a creaking wheelbarrow
pregnant with chamomile stalks
and flowers.

He pauses
between the glistering curtains of
hung fish, next to a translucent box
decorated with waning

candles that kneel
to touch the feet of a perpetually
crucified Jesús inside, his head
slung as if tired.

The man shifts
the weight of the load onto his
left side, releases his other hand
to cross his chest. He quickly kisses
two fingertips

alight
and presses them barely against
the glass: ashen prints on the dim
reflection of my forehead.
I could say

I understand
longing, but the truth is I know
nothing of his. At the corner,
I'm trading my coins for a bag
of yucca sticks;

                they remind
me of the snow and birch trees
lingering through another country's
winter—

                A story
at the hem of his story, all
I can say is that he might have
glimpsed back.

SELF-PORTRAIT AS SISTER

Sister, for you I've made a world within this poem's mouth,
since each mouth was created for constellations
of desire. In this poem, our general biographies
haven't changed: we were still born in one land,
raised in another, and live in cities perpetually
foreign to us. Because there's nothing wrong with that.
But in here, our supple tongues weren't raised measured by how close
our Englishes sounded to "the real thing." Here our tongues are proud
maps that guide us back to ourselves. Here we aren't sent whitening face
masks of cactus extract and lemon oil (only moisturizing ones) by Korean aunts
concerned about our darkening skin tones, our unabashed flirting
with the sun. Here people's kindness doesn't deny
who we are. Here we aren't set apart
at customs, led like lambs to a gray room at the back,
where officers are numb with suspicion and the air is stagnant from travelers,
families, holding their breaths and onto the warm sweat of each
other's hands as the seconds turn them colder.
In this poem, they are not there either,
and none of us have missed our connecting trains or worried
any friends. Here, sister, you don't cry while clutching at the phone,
as if it were the unraveling, pastel-pink comfort
blanket we used to share as babies. Aloneness hasn't driven us
into pining for a life where we try to fit into a shoe box
of a country, and our differences haven't made us
smaller in the squinting gaze of others. Here I promise
no love will end in assimilation. It'll just not
end. Here I don't wish us belonging. I wish us
the benediction of bell flowers and bees
and beloveds who'll hum with us sleepy songs.
I wish us here and beyond this poem: here, sister, here.

PRELUDE

I don't deny it. I've taken the dagger
of my tongue and gently
run it over your ear. I've often

thought *Umma*, said *Mother*, thought
it wasn't my mother whom I'd spoken about—
no one seemed to care.

I've whispered to my crushes, Te *quiero*, while actually meaning,
I want you. I had to use a Japanese word, *gingko*, to explain
in English my first time seeing the splitting yellow
fans of *eun-haeng* leaves in Korea.

There's so much of the past in these
choices; I doubt we'll ever fully understand each
other. Still, I wished for a long, unfractured life:
    In the spirit of superstition,
        I stubbornly slurped noodles, threaded needles.
    But again and again I dreamt
        I was a series of footprints
            pressed deep into the earth, covered in snow.

I was scared, so I told my parents about it, saying:
    나는 hilo의 삶을 바랬어요
        조심스럽고 잘리지 않게 자라고싶었어요. 하지만 soñé
  que me había vuelto muchos 발자국들, 땅에 깊이 눌려진 발자국들,
        cubiertos de nieve.

Do you trust what I'm saying? You can
trust me, just in the beginning. Then translate
me for yourself, question me

unsparingly like a sparrow
to another sparrow about breadcrumbs.

Notes

The word *Asterism* may refer to a pattern of stars observed by the naked eye or to a group of three asterisks (⁂). The opening epigraph in this book comes from Italo Calvino's novel *Invisible Cities*, translated by William Weaver.

(Dis)ambiguation [Before immigrant, noun] quotes from *For Nirvana: 108 Zen Sijo Poems*, written by Cho Oh-hyun and translated by Heinz Insu Fenkl.

Self-Study through Daily Sustenance was first inspired by Li Young Lee's poem "From Blossoms" in *Rose*.

El Milagro :: Edges borrows a line from Proverbs 14:10. El Milagro means the miracle in Spanish; it is also the name of a neighborhood at the north of Trujillo, Peru.

Self-Study through Homes found a guiding light in Etel Adnan's words from "Conversations with my soul (III)" in *Sea and Fog*.

Bougainvillea :: Papelillos: Just within Spanish, the Bougainvillea possesses several names. In Trujillo, the flowers are called Papelillo, which can be translated as Paperling.

Home Remedies includes a chant popular in Latin America sung to children who have injured themselves. Variations of this song exist depending on the region.

La Esperanza :: Poinciana Tree: Like El Milagro, La Esperanza is the name of a district at the north of Trujillo. It means the hope.

The quotes in **Self-Study through Prefixes** have been translated into English by Richard Sheldon and Esther Allen, respectively.

Drinking Alone After the Rain Stops was written after Li Bai's poem "Drinking Alone Beneath the Moon" (title translated by David Hinton).

Prelude's first epigraph "Traduttore, traditore," which can be translated into "translator, traitor," is an Italian saying that has often been employed to imply the impossibility of rendering an absolute translation. The second quote comes from Olena Kalytiak Davis's poem "Perhaps By Then You Will No Longer Be In Love" in *And Her Soul Out Of Nothing*.

Acknowledgements

I am grateful to the editors of the following journals, in which versions of these poems first appeared:

The Adroit Journal: "Bongsung-a :: Impatient Balsam", "Madrugada :: Small Hours", and "Prayer"
Arkansas International, "Sijo :: Genealogy"
Colorado Review: "Trujillo :: Homecoming"
Crab Orchard Review: "Dream Series of my Mother making Kimchi in Trujillo"
Ecotone: "(Dis)ambiguation [America]" and "Home Remedies"
Frontier Poetry: "Inheritance :: Invocation" and "Anything You Can Find in the World You Can Find in the Body"
The Georgia Review: "Self-portrait as my Mother," "Chicago :: Re-entry Ritual," "Road Trip," "Korea :: Things to Review Before Landing," and "Mending of Shoes"
New England Review: "Asterism," "When a Language is Said to be Lost," and "Self-portrait as I"
Nimrod International Journal, "Mogyoktang :: Inside"
Notre Dame Review: "Papers" and "Drinking Alone After the Rain Stops"
Pleiades: "Self-Study through Prefixes"
Poetry Magazine: "Conversation with Immigration Officer," "Prelude," "Self-Study through Homes," "Self-Study through Daily Sustenance," and "Green Card :: Evidence of Adequate Means of Financial Support"
Far-Near: "Grounding Exercise"
Poetry Northwest: "On Borders" and "(Dis)ambiguation [Occasionally]"
Small Orange Journal: "Han-sum :: Breath, Singular"
Southeast Review: "El Milagro :: Edges" and "Hyu :: In-Between"
The Southern Review: "Upon Practicing a Second Language"
Wildness: "Mercado Central :: Marginalia"
Yalobusha Review: "Self-portrait as Portrait"

A number of poems in this collection have also been printed as part of *Connotary*, a chapbook published by Bull City Press in October 2021.

A thousand thanks and more to Brenda Cárdenas, Cameron Awkward-Rich, Francisco Aragón, Ilya Kaminsky, Johannes Göransson, Joyelle McSweeney, Liam Callanan, L. S. Klatt, Mauricio Kilwein Guevara, Orlando Menes, Patrick Donnelly, Rebecca Dunham, Rosebud Ben-Oni, and Victoria Chang for their guidance and encouragement that have often saved me from my insecurities.

To Alessandra Simmons, Brett Hanley, Diana Cao, heidi andrea restrepo rhodes, Ina Cariño, Keith Wilson, Margaret Ray, Preeti Parikh, and Rachael Uwada Clifford for their thoughtful comments and companionship.

To the Tupelo Press team, Jeffrey Levine, Kristina Marie Darling, David Rossitter, and to John Murillo for seeing *Asterism*.

To Alethea Tusher, Kattia Quintanilla Castro, Esther Funez Castro, Hyeyoung Ahn, Siwar Masannat, and Young Kwang Park, every friend at each crossroad, the hermanas and hermanos in El Milagro, La Esperanza, and Trujillo, my families in Korea, Appa (이상기), Umma (김성희), Sin Hee Lee, and Daniel Jaeyoung Lee for gifting me the honor of being part of their lives and making these poems possible.